Lots of things to find and colour at Christmas

Designed and illustrated
by Stella Baggott

Written by Fiona Watt

There's a little white
mouse like this on
every double-page.
Can you find it?

D0505011

Find the all the snowmen wearing patterned hats and colour in their noses.

Can you find all the birds hiding between the snowmen? Colour them red.

2

Find the snow cats and bears wearing scarves and colour the scarves in bright colours.

03

Find the children carrying two presents and colour the presents red.

Can you spot the child with no presents?

Find one child holding five presents, then colour in the presents.

Find the children carrying three presents and colour the presents green.

Can you find six penguins holding Christmas stockings?

Find the white Christmas trees and colour them green.

6

Look for four penguins wearing reindeer antlers.

Can you spot a penguin decorating a Christmas tree?

Find the finished face in each row and colour it in.
Then, complete the other faces in the row.

Find the trees with four decorations on them and colour them in.

Find the trees with pots and colour the pots red.

Find the tree with a star on top and colour the star yellow.

9

Each little picture has a matching partner. Find the partner and colour it to match.

Can you find the picture which doesn't have a matching partner?

Find and colour all the angels holding trumpets.

Can you spot a candle with no flame? Draw a flame on it.

12

Find another candle like this one and colour them both red.

Find all the owls wearing scarves and colour the scarves in bright colours.

Can you find the owl which is still awake? Colour it in.

14

Find another owl the same as this and colour it in.

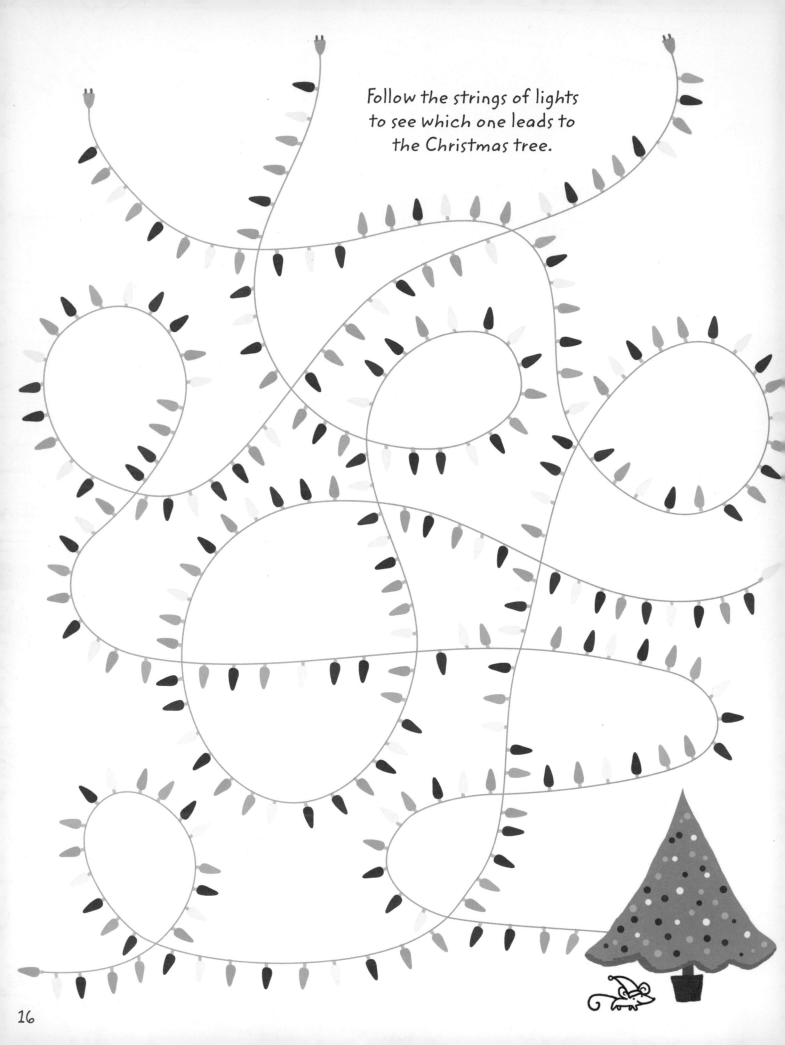

Follow the strings of lights
to see which one leads to
the Christmas tree.

Find all the birds and colour them blue, then find the squirrels and colour them orange.

18

Find the flowers and colour them red, then find the owl and colour it in too.

Look for all the white candy canes and draw red stripes on them.

Can you spot six mice eating gingerbread men?

20

Can you spot a mouse wearing a blue hat?

Find all the white presents and colour them in.

21

Find the animals holding presents and colour them in.

Colour in the animals wearing hats, too.

22

Find the odd-one-out in each row and colour it in.

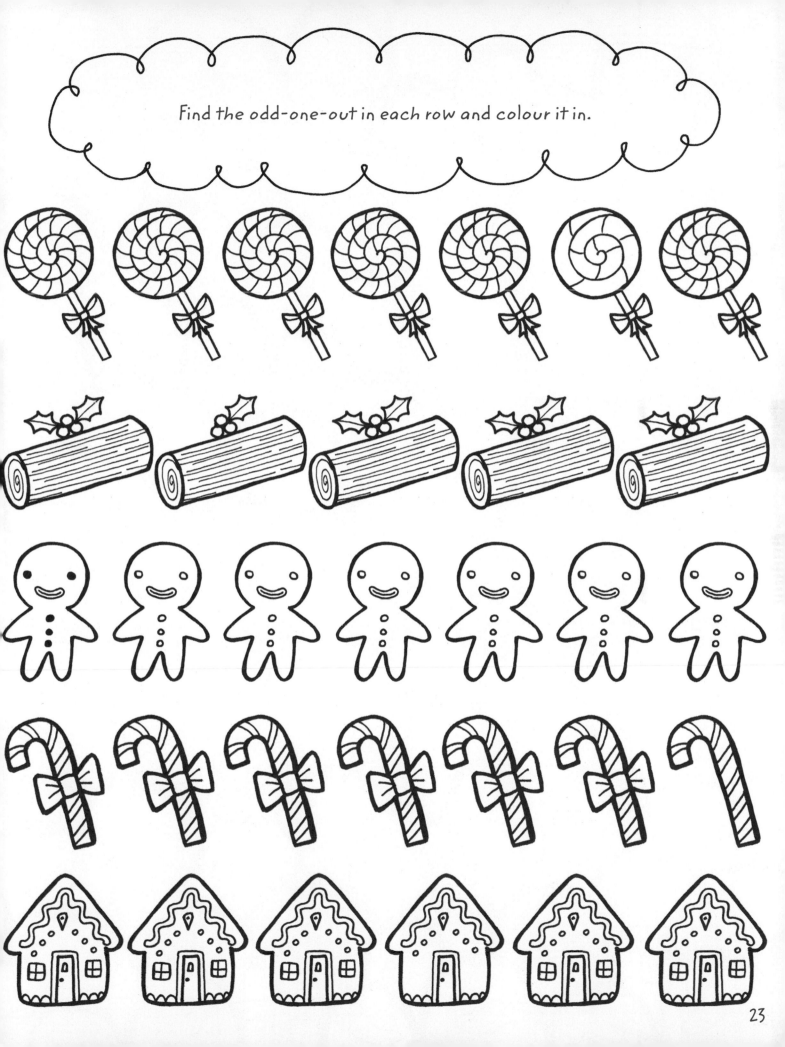

23

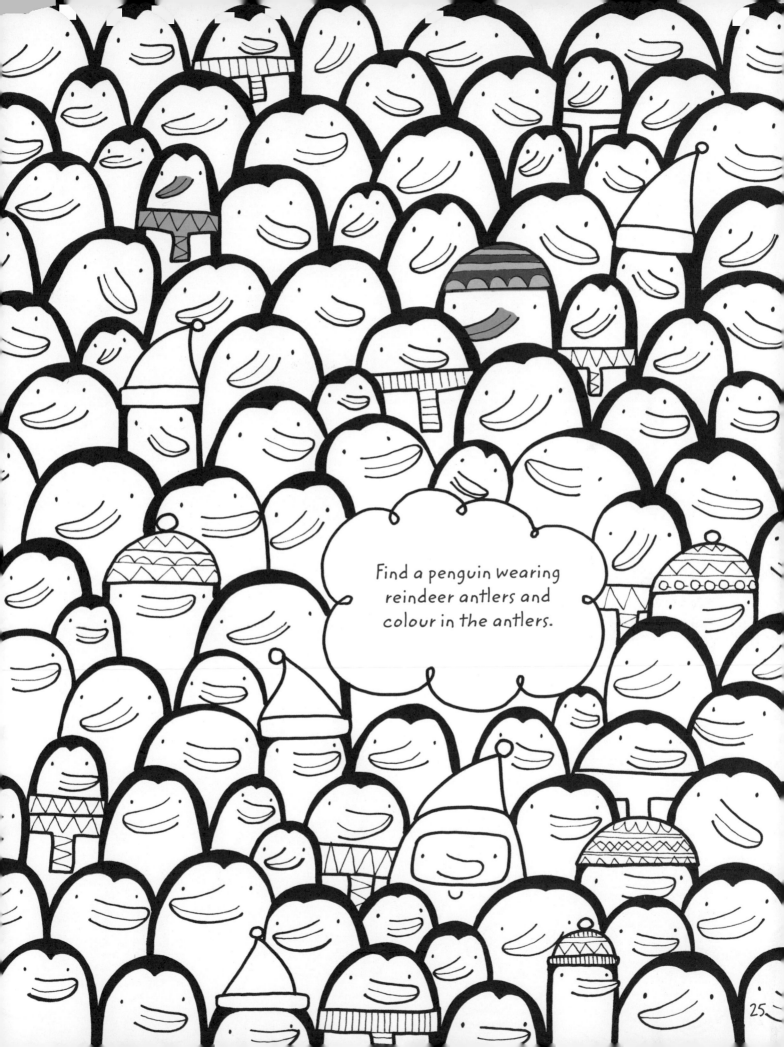

Find a penguin wearing reindeer antlers and colour in the antlers.

Find the sets of three matching dolls and colour them to match.

How many dolls
can you spot
that have birds
on their dresses?

27

Can you spot a
tree with four
cats sitting in it?

Find the sleeping
cats and colour
them orange.

28

Find a cat wearing a bow tie and colour it in.

Find all the cats wearing Santa hats and colour the cats and the hats.

Colour in the rabbits.

Follow the pawprints to see which rabbit
has eaten Snowman's nose.

30

Find all the snowmen with three buttons and colour in their hats.

Can you find a snowman with a bird on his hat?

31

Find five reindeer on skis and colour the skis red.

Find two reindeer eating candy canes and colour them in.

32

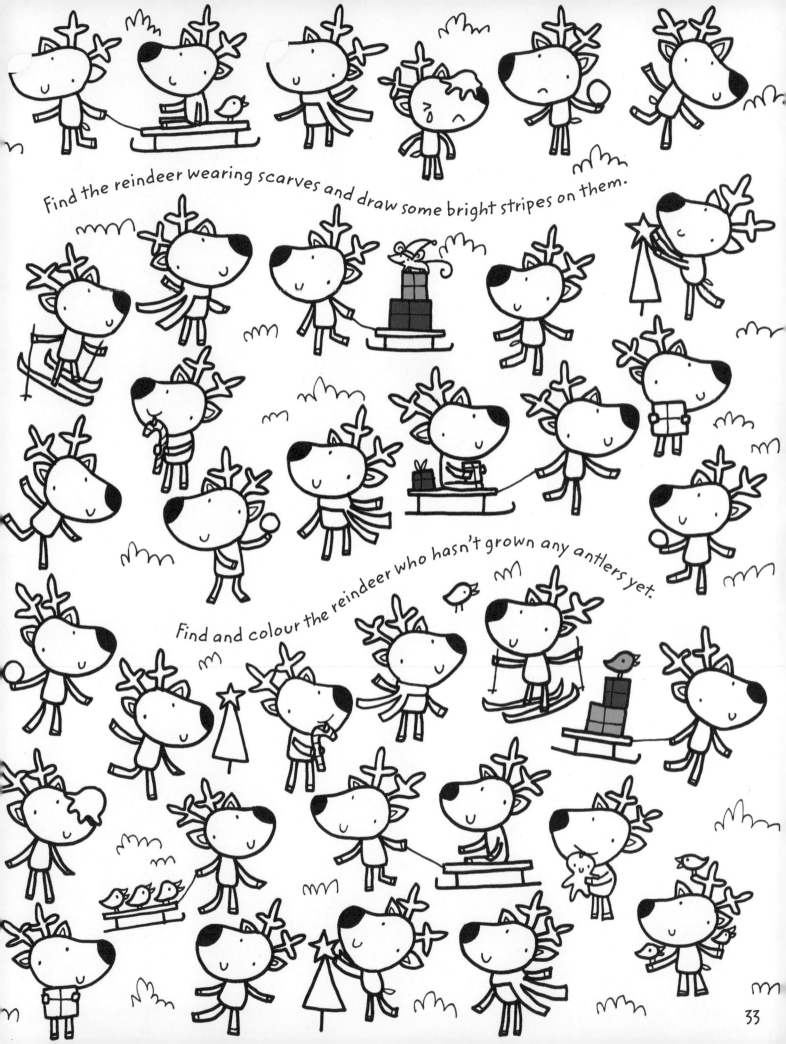

Find the reindeer wearing scarves and draw some bright stripes on them.

Find and colour the reindeer who hasn't grown any antlers yet.

Find six white candy canes and give them stripes.

Can you spot six gingerbread men wearing Santa hats?

34

Find six white lollipops and colour them pink.

This cupcake has a pink cherry on top. Find six more.

Find three animals who have slipped over on the ice. Colour them in.

Find and colour all the scarves in bright colours.

36

Colour in the things that you think Mrs. Christmas would need to make a cake.

flour

eggs

raisins

Which skier will make it to the finish line without bumping into another skier?

Colour in all the skiers.

FINISH

Find and colour all the elves wearing stripy hats.

40

Can you find Santa dancing with the elves? Colour him in.

Find and colour all the dancing presents.

Find and colour all the presents.

Find the reindeer and colour them purple.

Draw decorations on some of the plain trees.

43

Find a car with three penguins inside and colour the car yellow.

Find a car with two snowmen and colour the car red.

Find all the presents and colour them in bright colours.

Find a car with two reindeer
and colour the car blue.

45

Follow the lines to find out which chimney Santa should go down to reach the Christmas stockings.

Find and colour all the Christmas tree cookies green.

Find and colour the gingerbread men wearing bow ties.

Find the gingerbread man wearing a Santa hat and colour the hat red.

47

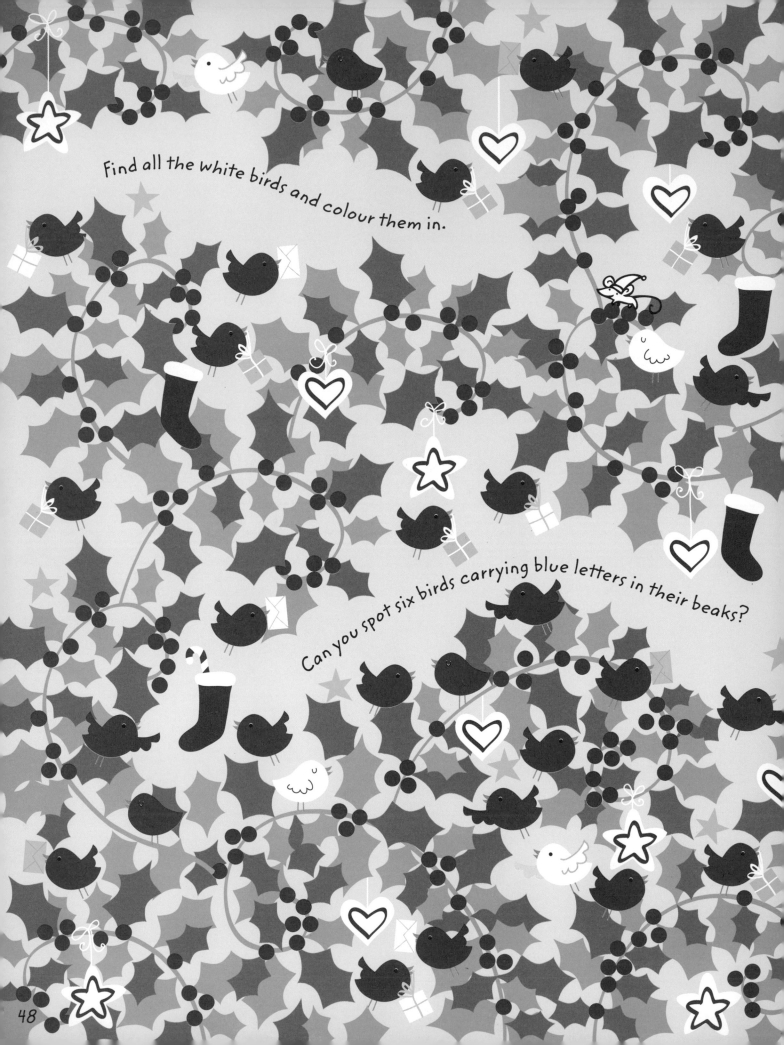

Find all the white birds and colour them in.

Can you spot six birds carrying blue letters in their beaks?

48

Find six white presents and colour them in.

Can you find a stocking with a candy cane inside?

Can you find a rabbit with a snowman on his jumper? Colour in the rabbit.

Find all the plain scarves and draw bright stripes on them.

Can you find the bear skiing among the rabbits? Colour in the bear.

50

Look for a rabbit who has lost its ski poles. Colour it in.

Find and colour all the rabbits with stripy scarves.

51

Find a Santa giving a carrot to a reindeer, then colour them in.

Can you find a Santa who has lost his hat? Give him a hat.

Find all the Santas building snowmen and colour them in.

Colour in the Santa putting a star on a little Christmas tree.

53

Find the stockings with trees and colour them green. Then, colour the ones with stars red.

Can you spot the stocking with a candy cane inside?

Draw patterns on all the plain stockings.

54

START
HERE

Draw a line through the maze to the middle of the snowflake.

Find the star-shaped decorations and colour them in.

Can you spot a decoration with a Christmas stocking on it? Colour in the stocking.

56

Look for the bird-shaped decorations and colour them in.

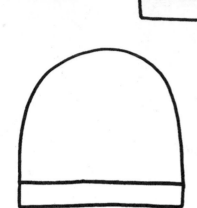

Find the snow globes with snowmen inside and colour in their hats and noses.

Draw pictures and snow inside the empty snow globes.

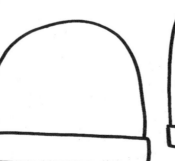

58

Can you spot a globe
with two rabbits inside?
Colour its base red.

Colour in all the things that you think might belong to Santa.

Draw a line to show the way Santa should fly
through the stars, back to his workshop.

Find all the
fairies carrying
presents and
colour their
dresses red.

Find all the fairies
wearing crowns
and colour their
crowns pink.

Find the fairies
with wands and
colour their stars
yellow.

Can you spot a
fairy carrying a
Christmas stocking?

63

Can you find and colour five white presents?

Spot a mouse carrying four presents.

Can you spot four hippos?

Can you find six reindeer?

Find six more snowflakes like this and colour them blue.

Draw some patterns on the plain snowflakes.

Find three big snowflakes like this and colour them to match.

Draw some snowflakes of your own to fill the spaces.

Find the odd-one-out in each row and colour it in.

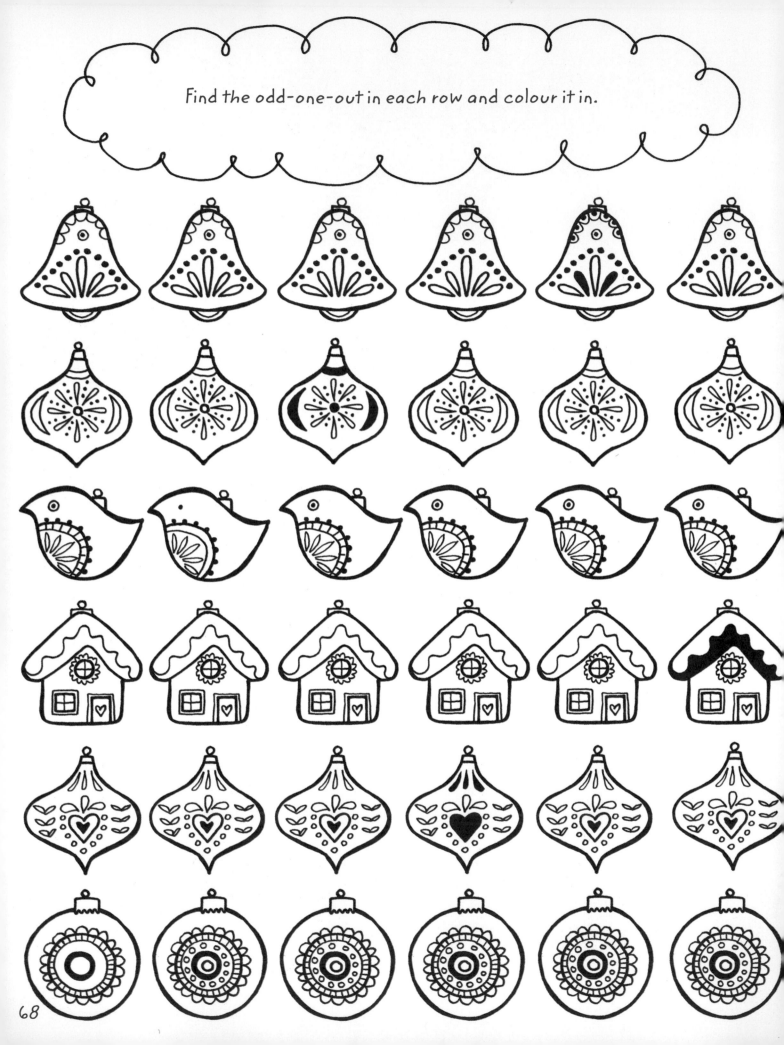

Find the gingerbread men and colour them brown.

Find the stockings and colour them red.

Colour the presents blue.

Colour all the stars yellow.

Can you find six lollipops? Colour them red.

Find twelve stripy sweets and colour them in bright colours.

71

Find all the stripy hats and colour them green.

Can you spot an elf who forgot to put his hat on?

72

Find all the presents and colour them in bright colours.

Find the snowmen and colour their noses orange.

Find the matching pairs of birds and colour them the same.

Which bird does not have a matching partner?

74

Look for the present hidden in the picture and colour it in.

Find each matching pair of gloves and colour them to match.

Then, look for the matching pairs of socks and colour them in, too.

Follow the lines to find out
which animal has dropped
their hat.

Find six bears wearing reindeer antlers.

This bear is holding a stocking. Find six more.

Can you find six bears wearing Santa hats?

Can you find six white bears and colour them in?

Merry Christmas

Find six more reindeer like this hiding in the picture.

79

Find and colour all the houses with smoke coming out of their chimneys.

Find the plain houses and draw on windows and doors.

Can you spot the house with someone looking out of the window?

Can you find another house exactly the same as this one?

Find the odd-one-out in each row and colour it in.

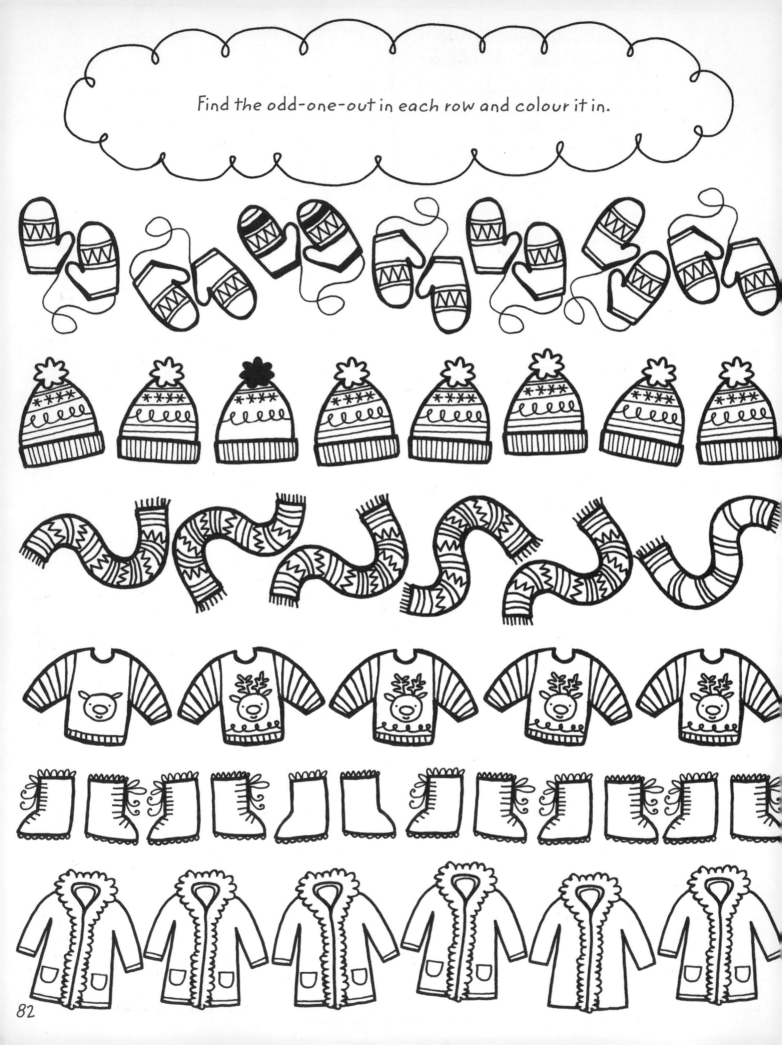

Draw a line along the swirly branches that the mouse should take from the top to the bottom of the Christmas tree.

START

FINISH

Find and colour
three little birds.

Find a bear wearing boots and
a hat, then colour them in.

84

Find the animals wearing scarves and colour their scarves in bright colours.

Can you find a sledge with two bears? Colour it in.

85

Colour in all the things that could be used to decorate the Christmas tree.

Find the stripy stockings and colour them in.

Find and colour the robins wearing hats.

Can you find a sleeping robin? Colour it in.

87

Find six more snowmen like this one, wearing blue earmuffs.

Can you spot six more bears wearing red scarves?

Find six white birds and colour them red.

Look for six more snowmen wearing green scarves like this one.

Can you spot six brown rabbits hiding behind snowmen?

89

Find the reindeer
with no antlers and
colour them brown.

Can you spot a reindeer
wearing a scarf?

Find and colour the
reindeer with presents
on their backs.

Spot the reindeer
with a red nose.

90

Find the odd-one-out in each row and colour it in.

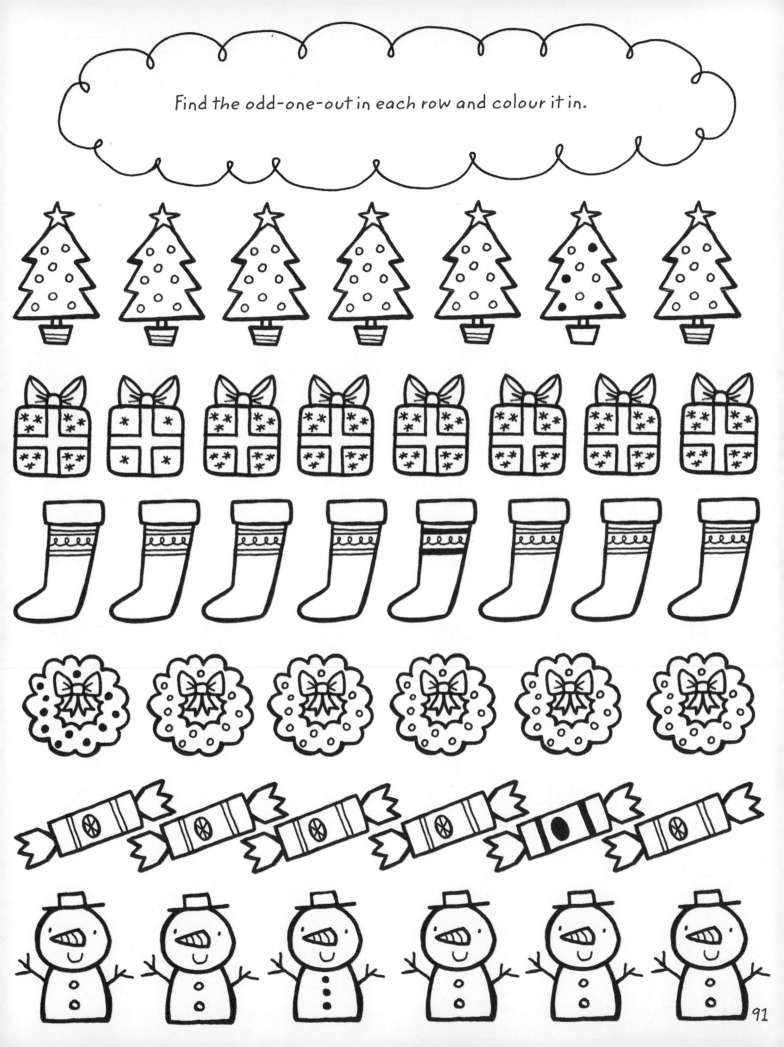

Can you find a holly
berry wearing a hat?
Colour in the hat.

Find all the sleeping holly
berries and colour them red.

Can you spot a star somewhere in the picture?

Find and colour all the singing birds.

93

Can you find another stocking exactly the same as this one?

Find six stockings with Christmas trees on them.

94

Draw patterns on all
the white stockings.

Find all the spotty presents and colour them red.

Find three presents that have red bows. Colour them in.

Draw patterns and bows on the plain presents.

First published in 2011 by Usborne Publishing Ltd., 83-85 Saffron Hill, London, EC1N 8RT, England. www.usborne.com
Copyright © 2011 Usborne Publishing Ltd. The name Usborne and the devices ♀ ⊕ are Trade Marks of Usborne Publishing Ltd.
All rights reserved. No part of this publication may be reproduced, stored in a retrieval system, or transmitted in any form
or by any means, electronic, mechanical, photocopy, recording or otherwise, without prior permission of the publisher.